J Sam is the author of three published works of full-length poetry, including *Bitter Wears a Smile* and *Every Man Jack of Us.* He is an educator, a socially conscious citizen, and a subscriber to the notion that good, through perseverance, will win over evil (and those 'dumbed-down' by societal ignorance and their consequences).

The publication of this book is for the love and memory of my son,
James Anthony Taylor.

J Sam

AIN'T THIS A BITCH?

A Compendium of a Life, Unextraordinary (Abridged)

AUSTIN MACAULEY PUBLISHERS®
LONDON * CAMBRIDGE * NEW YORK * SHARJAH

Ordering Information
Quantity sales: Special discounts are available on quantity purchases by corporations, associations, and others. For details, contact the publisher at the address below.

Publisher's Cataloging-in-Publication data
Sam, J
Ain't This a Bitch?

ISBN 9798891559387 (Paperback)
ISBN 9798891559394 (ePub e-book)

Library of Congress Control Number: 2024920734

www.austinmacauley.com/us

First Published 2024
Austin Macauley Publishers LLC
40 Wall Street, 33rd Floor, Suite 3302
New York, NY 10005
USA

mail-usa@austinmacauley.com
+1 (646) 5125767

This is in acknowledgement of my wife, Linda, who has never stopped believing.

Table of Contents

The Prologue

"People," not just science, "Make the World Go Round," as we were reminded by 'The Stylistics' Philadelphia Soul vocal group, in America's 1970s.[1] The lyrics of this classic single entertained the notion that there existed inherent problems with city politics, economic equity on the national level, and a generational attitudinal shift, toward global population diffusion. Begging, evermore, our civic and personal attendance to what goes on 'outside' the life…that suburbs provide to the 'escapist' in us. Where disillusionment, in the capture of miscarriage toward others, flees urban [f]ire, onto the smoldering heap of suburban commandeer.

As true as it was then, today (decades since), it rings an even louder bell—the 'wether' a socioeconomic-political climate sounds—when 'people' are in play. When, evidentiarily is the likelihood that 'relationship,' in these equations, discomfit with irony, insult, and peccadillo (public and private), to wit: "Ain't this a bitch?" be our riposte.

Not intended, by any means, as an exposé on the 'disputed' truth about what past, present, and future we have created for ourselves, thus our country, it is more an allusion to what 'uncommon' sense we [many] employ, while "surviving the drive" on a lifelong road, pockmarked with people who care only about time aggrieved, while traveling to and fro day to day.

Poetry…the music I make
Because I cannot sing.

J Sam
– 2024

---

[1] *Reference to the song 'People Make the World Go Round' by The Stylistics, on the album by the same title (1971).*

Woman

Feminized
Penalized
Brutalized
Terrorized
Ghettoized
Demonized
Scandalized
Circumcised
Traumatized
Compromised
Politicized Neutralized
Generalized Demoralized
Criminalized Destabilized
Illegitimized Antagonized
Hospitalized Eulogized

Eating 'American'; Today's Menu †††

Turkey & Dressing   Ham & Eggs   Grits & Red-Eye Gravy   Fish & Chips
Sauerkraut & Bratwurst   Corn Beef & Cabbage   Spaghetti & Meatballs

Sushi & Rice   Egg Foo Young & Gravy   Borscht & Pirogi   Gyros &
Tzatziki Sauce   Chicken Curry & Rice   Tamales & Coffee   Shish Kebab &
Piyaz Salad   Butter Croissants & Chocolate   Peanut Butter & JellyMac &
Cheese   Chicken & Waffles   Frybread & Three Sisters Stew

Apple Pie à la mode

††† Caution is advised for those with food allergies borne of severe cultural biases. Bigots Beware!

Damn Dreams!

In daydreaming,
What travels along the seams, this put-together life
Of rips, tears, breaks, and fractures.
        Put thus and so,
As "'the *ups and downs* of roller coasters,
    'the *ins and outs* of tides (where no sea willingly rolls),
    'the to's and fro's of 'times-a-changing' when standing still,
    'the NO PANKING! spot in esse's **PARKING**⇨,
    'the *back and forth* to Mother's house we [and I'm taking the children!] go,
    'the *off again on* again, desire's wanderlust,
    'the *D and R* but never *N* our social *P RNDL,*
    'the *zig-n-zag,* this dodgeball life what 'bullets' would not miss,
    'the *don't fence me in* of building fences,
    'the *here there and everywhere* annoyance of others' play,
    'the *side-by-side* display of oneness in crowds,'"
Oblige our un-amusement
At amusement
Parks.

From Plymouth Rock to Here

At the confluence of Montana Cool[2] and Dakota Pluck[3],
Contumacious[4] Wyoming trickles in, to forge a river.
Steeped in the red brine of salty old men,
Long since gone
To mulch the family tree of saltier-still 'ordinary folk.'
Disobedient to the custom and common,
The less unassailable branches.
Strong in the fruit they bear.
And suspicious about impressionable twigs
And broken limbs.
Season seems to little care,
That, not unlike a plantlife-major, uncertain, is this *wood*.

"Trees Are People, Too!"

---

[2] **cool**
/kool/
adjective: showing no friendliness, nor enthusiasm for [certain] people and [certain] ideologies.

[3] **pluck**
/plək/
noun: exhibiting nerve [to a fault] against the general public.

[4] **contumacious**
/känt(y)oo'māSHƏs/
adjective: acting out [willfully] against established [and universally acknowledged] authority.

Modern Art

Tattooed cutie!
Where **did** you go
When ink 'b' **came** your lover?
That 'h'ar**t which** once was mine,
Gave your las**t patch of** vacant skin
To the ar**tistic prose of a** joker.
Wh**o cou**ldn't **care** less
About your 'h'art, **engraved on** me, seems yesterday,
When *'I'* **was y**our canvas.
When *'I'* was the **targe**t of Cupid's duplicity.
Before your full bo**dy** laid down for *him*,
Convinced *you* that *I* **wa**s not your love of art,
But only **the** *"doodle"*
Of some**thing** *you* did not.

Askin' Jesus

They be dancin'
        Like the *Great Flood* never happened!

Forty days-n-nights,
And they be dancin' *the boogie-woogie*,
        Jerkin' *The Jerk*;
        Swingin' freestyle
Like nary a drop of rain
Ever fell on 'em!

Forty days-n-nights.
And for excess, they go…
        Stompin' on roses
Along the way to thorns.

And now,
        Contemporarily,
Verily into their rhythmic
        'Babylon Bounce,'
'F'ed are they…
        Literally!

Could be the reason why,
        Maybe,
The lion's share of 'em,
You know, the two-legged ones,
        Go about on two left feet
(Wing-tipped or stiletto),
But keep askin' to dance,
        That 'wallflower' not be
        Their virgin rite.

Socially 'Internetted'

Cain't be like no glamour queen.
Them folks I seen dressin' like 'em.
Talkin' like 'em.
Plumpin' lips
     And boostin' up their titties like 'em.

I, ain't them!
     Ain't!
     Are not!
       Cannot!
         Won't!

Jus' look at that blonde-headed, blue-eyed Black girl!
Blacker'n berries in vanilla cream.
     Wantin' some white man say she nat'rel.
       Fresh as mornin' sunrise.
     Jus' a-glowin' and a-waitin' his capture.

Jus' look at that cornrowed, black-eyed White girl!
Bobblin' head, manicured claws, surgical booty.
     Talkin' shit like *she* the shit!
     Tellin' some Black man he 'better reckonize!'
Jus' a-flossin'[5] and a-treshrin' what *he* done found.
     In her!

Naw, cain't be like no glamour queen.
     Already got 'nuff no-good mirror 'flections
     Trying to make me somethin' diff'rent
     Than what I am.
And I ain't!

---

[5] *American slang, meant to characterize a person as showy and overly adorned in expensive appearance.*

Integrated

Something *'mensch'*
About [this] basket of fruit:
>   Juxtaposed homogeneity by race, class,
>   National origin.
>   '[Those] people'—judged.
Segregated with kind by shape and size.
>   Color.
And other dis-similarities predisposed.

[This] basket, [this] *'mensch'* camaraderie:
>   Cornucopia-attached, fragrant and recombinant.
Beckons many a hand into its mien,
>   The touch, taste, texture of fruit,
>   Nibbled, nibbled, nibbled
On frenzy of tongues, so many palates pleased.

[These] apples, oranges, grapes.
[These] agents provocateur,
The promulgation of *Mixed Fruit*.
>   Whose sexy pear curves,
>   Whose suggestive banana,
>   Whose titillating peach, chin-dripping,
>   Spark the passion for eating,
>   And makes little effort to deny

>   The multicultural bent
>   Of credenzas,
>   Coffee tables,
>   And countertops.

[This] instance, where 'size' *does* matter,
>   'Color' matters.
'Difference' matters.
>   Collocates appetite:
>   Visual, tactile, olfactory.
>   That divides the succulent sweet,
>   From the *seedy* nature of sour
>   Grapes.

Thus, on composition of *the assorted,*
>   Still Art claims 'nonsectarian.'
Multicultural-interracial neighboring,
>   Those basket friends.
>   Mingling, touching.

Cohabitating their wicker, wood, glass accommodations
          —Plastic, in environs less upwardly mobile—
Makes prone, the paucity of *Fresh Produce*,
          Transitory, at best.

[This] basket.
[This] aggregate sweet-n-fleshy.
[This] *Promethean* dichotomy,
          'Rich,' the luster of some;
          'Poor,' the darkening, daily,
               The many.
Lays siege upon [this] grinding plane,
          Public and Private a land,
With dietary proclivity t'ward polarized
          Fruit cups.
                    Lunch boxes.
                         Snack packs.

Bodes, unwell,
For less-popular pomes
          And nut fusion,
Apposite to waste,
          And appetite lost.

What the U.S. Declaration of Independence Said... 'A Footnote History'

Didn't say *nothing* 'bout racial profiling;[6]
Didn't say *nothing* 'bout marginalization;[7]
Didn't say *nothing* 'bout socio-economic bias;[8]
Didn't say *nothing* 'bout voter suppression;[9]
Didn't say *nothing* 'bout racial/partisan gerrymandering;[10]
Didn't say *nothing* 'bout ex-felon disenfranchisement laws;[11]
Didn't say *nothing* 'bout redlining;[12]
Didn't say *nothing* 'bout voter caging;[13]
Didn't say *nothing* 'bout excessive voter purging;[14]
Didn't say *nothing* 'bout voter intimidation;[15]
    And definitely
Didn't say *not a damn thing!* about being Black, while breathing.[16]
    Least ways,
    Nothing *of worth*,
    Repeating.

---

[6] *The policy practice of stereotyping certain groups in order to enforce unequal protection by law enforcement.*

[7] *Pushing people to the fringes of society by making it difficult for them to achieve equal status in society.*

[8] *Disadvantages imposed upon certain groups to keep them in negative social and economic situations.*

[9] *Any number of methods used by the party in power, particularly at state and local levels, to ensure the difficulty of certain groups in exercising their right to vote.*

[10] *Occurs when the dominant political group tries to change a voting district to negatively affect a group they do not favor.*

[11] *The practice of prohibiting ex-felons from access to the vote even when all enfranchisement requirements by law have been met.*

[12] *The practice of denying loans to certain neighborhoods on a discriminatory basis according to race or ethnicity.*

[13] *The practice of political parties or organizations of using the mails to solicit unlikely supporters, anticipating that those mails that are deemed as 'undeliverable' can legitimately be removed from the voter rolls.*

[14] *The practice by state and local governments of removing citizens from voter rolls for a variety of nefarious, self-serving reasons.*

[15] *Defined under the law as threats, coercion, and attempts to intimidate for the purpose of interfering with the legal right of a person to exercise his/her vote.*

[16] *Expression from, among others, "Breathing while Black: Rude and Frightful Encounters With Police [,] Recalled By Distinguished African Americans, 1860–2012," Robert Fikes Jr., Jun 30, 2012, Journal of Pan African Studies (Vol. 5, Issue 5)*

Sugar Daddy

Men who create
　　Time after time
Women's dependence on fossils
　　As fuel
And on men who become them
　　And it

Men who gestate
　　In women's labor
The ownership issue
　　Of *body*
And on laws it becomes
　　By men

Men who conflate
　　In value and scheme
The parchment by reams
　　A court *Supreme*
Deliberates
　　Women

Public Opinion's Court

Obsequious in her attentiveness
        My mendacity's habit,
She attended, but perspective of family,
        Friend, neighbor, and stranger.
Who, perjurers all
        About my doings,
Averred knowledge of me
        More than mine!

And they

The People

v.

Found me

The Defendant

Guilty!

[*Hereby sentenced to razor-wire whispers, desolate in solitude's self-absorption;
Insinuated in rumor's mill, the likes of lepers and bill collectors,
And others disinvited to silence.*]

"Nigga!"

What the paint does not wash white,
Are scribbles left in permanent marker.
Not by unruly children,
But by men,
Undergrown
To sensitivity about their naked necks.
Reddened by the idea
That '*racist*' fetches
A clodpole's embrace.

"...Of the People, by the People, and for the People"[17]

"A basket for your head, sir?" She proffered,
 Of smile what pulled him t'ward her ample bosom.
  A place o' visual recompense,
   Bedecked in nature's jewels—sweet perspire
    Strung down her youth,
Into the valley of her concern for bloodletting
  On so public a ground.

 'Nay, fair mistress, permit my bedeviled head to roll
  Upon the gutter!
 Away, all maidens' exigency
  Of my iniquitous affairs.
 Caused me to this scaffold
 Above you mob, cuckolds among you,
  What cheers bestow upon me,
   This fate, for molestation I did
 Upon the hearts and minds, the gullible.
  Nubile and not!
 Upon whom I averred true love.
 While carnal,
  My true intent.'
"So be it your final word, our presence, sir?"
 Asked caution's note, her whisper.
Of robust mouth—wet—her unwilted breath,
 Told truths unquietly to the damned,
 Roused in rabble, the living.

 'What purpose serve this center town?
 That, unshuttered be my gaping proclamations.
 If not for its people gather 'round
  The carnage that is my life,
   Circular on display
   Amidst a linear moral
    Turpitude.
 What beast be beast!
  If not its prowl provoke the social ire
   The innocent of heart?
    Decent, in their running wild
   The ways of the wood.
 And by their cheer, do agree,

---

[17] *From Abraham Lincoln's 'Gettysburg Address,' November 19, 1863.*

This decapitation my mortal soul
From this [re]public place.
And I am hellbound to see it through!
…This "justice" be on fornicators.
But surely upon its men—free
The "virtue" of chastity locked.

'Give onto my face, what you see me now.
…This deluge, the rot of cabbage and tomato spite.
This "boo" and "hiss,"
That I am full the waste of tables
In defective home-keeping.
To have made oddment so many a maiden,
Under spell of my appetite
For famished womanhood.

'Just as I have rendered you!
Whore-like in duty,
Into my imperfect pedigree.

'Loose my head upon this square!
To privilege your soured and dirty stone cobbles.
Your mud, your piss,
Your bowel defiled.
As have I, your blackened hearts.'

Which, to *that*,
Stone to stone, his careening dome.
In sow's slop,
Full-stop!

Hero Worship
The Art of Aging Well

Forever young!
Until you are not
The destiny that unfolds
After having done a lifetime's laundry.
Whose suds tell stories of *all and sundry*
What soil there is in underwear
Worn by celebrity,
And folks other
Your approbation.

Scion upon scion,
Surge upon
The temptation to be *[un]like dear ol' Dad!*
Spun from home,
Slept on by revolutionary ethos
And other visitors,
For wine, dine, and conversation
Better rendered in theater.

Abet the faux paladin in you!
Beset on all sides by the 'good old folk' in dark clothing.
Blending in, mixing it up
With
Those, dressed in white, who refuse to see
The great equalizer that is *Time*,
In making 'old'
Even the fledglings among us.

Boston Cream Pie

Old World in *New World* tin.
Its branded footwear—briskly through—to and fro where tourists sit.
Some plump, some lean.
Walking, biking, driving.
Distinguishable most, by their German, Italian, and Japanese luxury mobility.
Upwardly
To their cosmopolitan milling about
The haute cuisine
Of health,
Wealth,
And the dis-acknowledgment that others also gather here.
Strapped to satchels, backpacks, totes, and slings.
Through Bostonian *Beaux Arts* and *Renaissance Revival,*
About the architectural relics, turned to gold,
That *have-nots* have not
The red cent of a dime's coffee.
Whose 'ne're do wells' limp and grovel, and importune a city's pardon,
For the 'fantasy' of famine among 'vagrants and pigeons'[18]
Who take the dole given, but to give it back
To the beggary of cheap spirits,

Cardboard lean-to living,
And 'such folly' that is *poverty*
And apathetic social contract.
Sitting where centuries have plopped them
And done little about their sidewalk stain,
What tarnish be their second-hand butts
And matted hair.
Putrid in their lower caste.
Unabiding of *law & order*liness,
While handcuffed to the guilt
Of addiction
To pie pan[handling].

Oh, that *all* do care!
But not enough to care *for.*

---

[18] *Reference to Boston Globe columnist Lawrence Harmon's article, "Boston Irish Famine Memorial Needs to be Restored," November 9, 2013, downloaded July 27, 2019.*

'Southern-Fried' Dixiecrat

Plutocrat, *Dixie*!
Aging Anglican, Pollyanna.
Reluctant mother of 'republic'…
    Those '*mammy*' types. Disguised in baptism.
    Submerged in the hot grease what by the name—*God*,
    Goes rampant, devil-may-care.

Who is more cavalier, still? Her *men*!
    Her rulers' chaotic roost…
    Cocksure as the capon.
    On occasion, the hen,
Whose populace caterwaul,
    "Our *daily bread* imperiled!"
Oft-repeats, thus and so, this way and that,
    'Down home' spun to kibble eaten by dogs.
                   And their lovers.
    And others so inclined 'serfdom of the mind'
                  Du jour.
(i.e., *Southern-fried Chicken Shit*!)

Jurisprudence, 'Jerry-Rigged'

Abort! Abort!
Abort the sanction flagship demagogues—'God chosen!' Make much, the decisions reserved for…*God*.
>Who, through woman, chooses
>>That *man* is wont deliberation
>>On matters such pertained to *her*.

Abort! Abort!
Abort the sanctimonious 'screws.'
>Who perforate prerogative
>With burdens[19] intended as tools.
>>Likely hammer, nail, and *plank*.
>Constructs and deconstructs so,
>>That warranty is impeached
>>For who owns the rights to *woman*.

Abort! Abort!
Abort the rats, the sinking ship *America*!
>"Great Again" its *never was*.
>>Never is.
>>Never will.
>>Never.

Abort! Abort!
Abort the albatross, *Conservative*.
>Whiplashed, on corrupted necks-n-notions
>Of censorious body collective,
>>By the bondage of a people,
>>Shackled to party
>>Politick.

---

[19] *Reference to "The White Man's Burden," a poem by Rudyard Kipling, regarding American imperialism, beginning with its occupation of the Philippines, after victory in the Spanish American War, written in 1899. And as some might say, imperialism starts at home, leaves the front door and becomes an oppressive nation.*

"Zebe!"

<u>I</u> am *Dick and Jane.*
That *'50s* rehash, the glory of *'Old.'*
When *'New'* gives me

                          Stars   stars
                  stars   stars stars
                stars   stars   stars
                      stars   stars,

And makes <u>your</u> *sttttttrrrriiiippppe*
             Universally,
          Undesirably *'Colored.'*

Be ***littled***—you *'zebra!'*
Your stripes shown for what man allows,
        With tornadic force thrust into the Savannah,
Where worms move Earth
          & Heaven
To keep <u>me</u> more
Preponderant.

The Pressure of 'Peer'

The diaspora of the less dutiful flock
Summons a bird to inquisition:
> *"How early, really were you,*
> *And what worm—unawares—found its way*
> *Into your 'peckish' disposition?"*

> *"Praytell,"* in Bird's response,
To his ineffectual delators:
> *"Why idle were craws like yours?*
> *Idle, more, the craws of your bird wives and bird young.*
> *Your 'untenanted care' their welfare?"*

"Pre—-posterous!" in unison, their rejoinder, Bird's retort:
> *"That you refrain aspersions-cast*
> *This winged body, with due respect!*
> *Conjecture goes to truth as fabrication,*
> *That in 'this' avian-worldly, do birds of a feather**
> *Resolve themselves to communal measure.*
> *Forestall decline, the nesting culture of avarice,*
> *The solitary!"*

> *"Balderdash!"* rebuked, indignant Bird.
> *"Of my feather, I do make this claim:*
> > *To countenance communal command, I cannot!*
> *Before my flock, my <u>nest</u> is due*
> > *What, foremost, duty is my lot.*
> *When community before family,*
> *Into reality's face, flies,*
> > *To tumult becomes maintenance.*
> *Misbegotten, in conclusions about eggs.*
> *And other things cracked*
> > *And broken.*
> *An inconsideration*
> *To salubrious nest you keep.*
> > *Whose anvil chorus forge complaint:*
> > > *[Hunger's unappeasable protest].*

There, it comes, the worriment,
What unwholesome design, a family distressed,
> *That kowtows to the squawking wings, a public,*
To the ruination of all things
Felicitous."

Discomfiture revealed!
>An inquisition, disarmed,
Hemmed and hawed the forfeiture, the catbird seat.

Until silence about the eloquent Bird:
>*"Lest 'tradition' wane, what others do,*
>*Gone are livelihoods,*
>>*The 'good eggs' of a feather!"*

The Rope Getters 😃

Another thing about lynch mobs…
    Their ropes. 😵

    Their tugging and towing judgment
    Tied to pickup trucks and tree limbs. 😠

And to their discontented suburban housewives—swollen
        In servitude to diminishing 'majority rule,'
            Losing numbers in their Exit
        Polls. 😮

And to their men—matrimonial in their alpha dispassion
        For the uncivil consequences
        Of brute resistance to difference. 😼
            Indifferent and disjointed
        In their confluence of rabble's sanctimonious river,
            Running through. 😖

            …And over,
            Their muddied banks. 😧

The Nativist-American

Shakespearean tragedy, staged within.
        Unconfined, shore to shore.
Coterie upon coterie, our small towns play
        What plots subplot *"The American Way!"*
           Archaic anew.
            Oft preposterous! but true.
        Presented us, the "bitches" and "brutes"
        Who are constant in their causes upon others' mortal wounds,
           To be called, 'exceptional!'
And we name the fallen, 'foreign.'
        "Delightfully Ethnic!"
This 'Irish luck' of leprechauns and lepers.
        "Provocative. Untouchable."
This wisdom in China's fortunate cookie
        And kung fu.
(Owing to zodiac gemstones that have nothing to do
        With food or fight.
Or what mamas and daddies did not teach
        Their children.)

Russian vodka.
        Scotch whiskey, upon these native shores.
Emboweled in yesteryear's Nordic pluck,
        Sea-worthy in their squat dance and bagpipe
        Upon Rio's *Carnival*, Havana's contraband leaf
           And America's Fourth,
        That consumption keep 'cultural'
           'Multi-.'

French Pastry proliferates,
        Upon,
        Within,
        Throughout
Canadian-slathered sugary sweet.
        Upon,
        Within,
        Throughout
The Alpine chocolate of *Swiss Movement's* time
        On Wall Street's ethnic wrists.

Or at their British-logo *high teas*,
    Where Dutch tulips sip with mid-day's Korean kimchi,
    Turkish kebabs,
    Italian pastas,
    And the Tea Garden—Frisco, Japanese.
    Dressed in button-down collars
At California-*cosmopolitan* sidewalk cafes
  And *Tapas!*

Nepalese Sherpas eat here, too.
    Their neighboring Mongolian *buuz*, all the rage!
    Among Mandarin potstickers and Polish perogies, that is.
    And **I.**ndian **P.**ale **A.**le as our *Rothschild's* drink.
      While breaking Israeli unleavened bread
      From Marrakech to Washington politics.
      From Germany's *brötchen* & *spätzle*
    And Austria's Viennese rye,
      To, none other than,
  Times Square street-cart pretzels & weiners.

Egyptian cotton—counted.
    And sarcophagi.
'Uptown,' 'Downtown.'
All-about-town, on display.
    Itinerant in curiosity, about 'ghettos' and 'hoods.'
    Peopled hallways of midnight
      [And other o'clocks where light does not go].
    Voiceless, about the erstwhile dioramas of the Indigenous,
      Swollen in lips of Africa's *mystique*
      Pressed prominently against a transparent wall,
      This Hollywood jungle, *Los Angeles*!
      Where we are feckless in our disregard
      For less advantage, the poor.
Portuguese grotto, off *First and Main.*
Where *'Flamenco Served Nightly'*
    The vacationist palate for red w/ruffles,
      And the gypsy ways
      Of dance's hidden secrets…
        "Olé!"
Curries favor with suburban Elm Street—India's *'namaste.'*
    Sudan's, Somalia's, and Syria's promise to pay
    What price, freedom.
Out of the tired pockets, our 'thankless' *America!*
  Branded "*Samaritan*," but crafted, that hegemony keep.

Brazil skewers churrasco,
  On U.S. Highway *'Restaurant Row.'*
    Near Third Street and Maple.

Caddy-corner from the five-and-dime that the jukebox built.
Where the buck didn't stop "here" for Truman,
Nor for celebrity awaiting *Discovery!*
Ashore by waves, *"dead in the water,"* upon amber's 'flooded' fields of grain.[20]
Up majesty's mountains, rocky and high,
The climb to *inclusion's* exclusion:
Vietnam pho, sucked aplenty from victory,
Into the polite prosperity

Of our 'conscientious objections'
To all things *Orient.*

Australian 'roo—African ostrich, too—plated,
Disperse among our custom of bison and beef.
Given in to, "but it's so tidy," the terraced rice and the sea's weed.
And the painted skin of Indonesia,
That beauty preoccupies,
The, time-and-again, ugly
Peopled-abodes of our neighborhoods,
Ornate or homespun in our ethno-centri-
Cities.

And we are casual in slippery sadiq—that Saudi black
And that Gulf Coast Mexico [crude]ness of polluted skies,
Berthed alongside Thailand's tree-rubber rage,
That our common intolerance to walking, be placated.
Reduced to **M**.iles **P**.er **H**.our
And the footprint of carbon, running
'Sea to dingy sea.'

Vindication!
"Our country tis of" Anglophone 'empire' claim
That *canceled*, is culture, this *nativist* land.

---

[20] Reference to *America The Beautiful*, by Katharine Lee Bates, published 1895; also with an indirect reference to John Denver's song, *Rocky Mountain High*, 1972.

Optics[21]

Roaches
Who scaled the walls
Like they did not care
Who was watching

Found their way
Into our *bread & butter*
Our **Cookie Jar**
Our Mom's apple pie

Left the kitchen in ruins
A nation henceforth hesitant
To eat

---

[21] *Refers to pictures and videos of hundreds of, who some refer to as domestic terrorists (outfitted in clothing with words like "freedom," "liberty," and "patriotism" prominently displayed), climbing the outer walls to breach America's capitol grounds and buildings from beyond; growling in dog snarls and hog grunts, upon their attack, on January 6, 2021. These images, according to some viewers, were reminiscent of rampaging insects, wildly about a feeding frenzy.*

D.I.V.O.R.C.E.

Widow's weeds—her wardrobe.
To celebrate a man who lived
        Vicarious in deeds of do-good men.
This man, these men,
Uncommonly she comes to grieve.
But only to bury miscalculations in *Time Served*
        "Loving,"
        "Honoring,"
        "Cherishing."

Becomes "No More!" this most common law, *Attraction*.
        "No More!" the **D**etachment,
        Exasperated by the chill of
                His wintry separations.
                Her calls for covers. On summers heat.
        "No More!" the **I**ncongruences,
        Conjoined piece by piece with
                His puzzling adaptations,
                Her imperfect pictures of his family value.
        "No More!" the **V**ociferous discounting
                Her time, cowering under the thunderclap
                His bluster invective.
                Her unmuffled protestations of 'patient' endurance.

        "No More!" the **O**bstreperous resistance,
                Her time. Beseeching a change,
                His ruination,
                Her matrimonial bliss;
        "No More!" the **R**ancor ensured,
                Her time recovering the broken
                His self-destruction given
                Her womanly predisposition.
        "No More!" the **C**ensorious reproach
                Her time, as wife and confidante
                His unctuous response
                Her uxorial duties;
        "No More!" the **E**vasiveness
                Her time, giving chance to love
                His self-regarding
                Her selfless approach to caring.

Widow's weeds—her wardrobe.
To celebrate a man who lived
      At odds, her 'finery' now appears:
          Incomplexity adorned
          In her accoutrements *untoward*.

The Sin of 'City'

Sidewalk spat from nasty night
Opine, like ass,
     Among the daylight's moving crowds.

Incivility stink
Sweats upon the great 'washed'
     That "**God Saves!**"
But seems not.

Good standing denizen.
     Crawl you, among them, tiptoe!
About what welfare this bramble
     —Public—
          Is unwell.
Whose dysentery runs Uptown,
     This Downtown corridor to Hell's Heaven.
          "Hoopla on the loose!"
          Obtuse!!!
          This crossroads seam—debauched!
Whose fabric, secrets keep
     Butt naked.
     Neon illustrated.
Whose ribald digest print, curb to curb,

     Notion's incoherent liquor remedies.
          [Loquacity²],
That good times be had by all.

There is no Mickey[22] here.
     But for the Finn,[23]
          What beyond a gullet goes
          Unchewed.
          Indigestible
          The hometown *family-friendly*.

---

[22] *Reference to the attraction of the Mickey Mouse® character at some of the world's renown theme parks, located particularly in California and Florida, USA.*
[23] *Reference to the 'Mickey Finn'—a drink laced with a psychoactive drug, or agent designed to incapacitate the recipient [who has been administered the drug without their knowledge]. A practice commonly referred to as "slipping someone a Mickey."*

Would it be?
Could it be,
That, along this concrete asphalt lane,
          This juggernaut cheer of misbehaved,
'Family,'
'Friends' are not?

The Fart

What, in half the public's opinion, matters,
When half does not either, matter,
Nor matter to have one?

That *other* half, I mean,
For whom matters of opinion
Are as butts, blessed to all.

So too, all,
Cause flatulent despair,
The foul inequity of breathable air.

The Florida State Fair
(circa 1953)

Let in,
The left-out swarmed upon *Negro Day*.
      That *[set-apart]* time,
      Against cross-contamination,
Mono-culture's benevolence.
      One, over Other,
      Under race's *Color Line*,
      The entrants.

Sliced watermelon.
      Popped corn
And shaved-ice cones,
      Colored, as the black hands that carried them,
Rode the rides.
Towed the line to '*Minority*.'
    Secondary, in their amusement at four hundred years
    Excluded.

And in all of 'one' day come,
      Deterred, they were not,
      This food and frolic extravagance.
This candy-apple, cotton candy-picking sugar-licking crowd,
      'Separate but Equal'

Upon the *Midway* sights and sounds
      That white folk make
When safeguarding the station in life,
        Theirs.

"I Ain't Shout'n."

Build that wall.
Keep them out.

Fire the cold, dark night by torch,
Predisposed to mob rule of boar,
    Wild in their willingness t'ward anarchy
Against "these huddled masses yearning to breathe…"
    In askance of liberty's flavor, but a morsel not
        To assuage the wrong done civility
        Upon 'those people.'

Build that wall.
Keep them out.

Flout what dysentery amass a country-wide,
    My ignoble disregard for that not White,
    Not Anglo-Saxon,
    Not Protestant.
    Not.
Exclaim what bent, is my 'yellow' daily report.
    My centuries-old chronicling,
        Disease! Mayhem! Debauchery!
    Fraught with "border thieves" upon our 'Sanctuary' cities.
        So vulgar, the mixing,
        A nation.

Build that wall.
Keep them out.

Stay lit the torrid flame, our discriminant predilections.
    Red-hot, in our Amendments.
        Our public policy.
        Our proposition of 'American' largess,
Curtailed by our 'Native' sleep
        On pillow-top and high-count linen
        Dreams.

Build that wall.
Keep them out.

Bay from rooftop to rabble roused,
     Upon these deafened ears,
That the *soul* of 'Nation' hears
     Nothing.
Build that wall.
Keep them out.

Spasmodic, beats
   My cathartic heart.

Gardening's 'Patch'

The Old...

Soil disturbed makes furrowed field.
Makes seed the possible miracle.
      The mark of *That* greater.
Becomes descendant—Man.

Barren, becomes ground unbroken.
Absents itself of labor's nutrient.
      What dearth of, make 'hard scrabble,'
Life less eaten.

That, itself, asserts to symmetry, those lines,
The order that *right* stands *up*—the offspring crop.
      Undrooping to family table,
For 'right to life,' its *Produce*.

Its loins result, are *Greens*—fertilized.
Homogenized in their sorted rows, as people.
      Segregated by color, taste, and texture.
'To weed or not...' by culture-norm or bias.

The New...

Privileged, to ripening.
To *heirloom*—deep-rooted.
      Suburb's proclivity for gardening 'salad,'
To *hybrid*, 'meat-eating,' City.

Sans diligent care, these *urban weed*,
These prickly bother of feral nurture
      And other such cultivated 'bounty,'
—Brings to wither, a ghetto's '*patch*:'

Mulish to gangly, its measure;
Nor food for comfort, its progeny.
      Entangled in *affairs of state,*
Where harvest yields fallow, a cupboard-bare REVEAL.

Disabused, this '*patch*,' of notion that [old] crows, scare,
Refused, it, too, the 'color, sheen, shine'[24] to vegetable *side dish*.
       Thus watered last, is its parched and brittle soil
By the hands of constant hunger.

---

[24] From Vegetable Harvest Time, "When to Pick Vegetables?" on things to look for in order to get 'wholesome' food from the garden to the dinner table.

Known By the Mirror,
Reflection Ignores

Vanity.
A mockery!
Foolish in fame.
Loin-clothed, scantily clad
       In adjectives conjectured, a *rose,*
       Thorny in its willingness to draw blood
       From the *turnip*, Beauty.

Vanity.
A *gilded* affront.
Ugly in truth, perfume-stinked
       In fragrant douche,
       The funk of lesser claims to *celebrity*
Worn thin in its braggadocio about favor
       By the unaesthetic *ordinary.*

Vanity.
Repeated offender.
Retroactive in nature,
Perfunctorily common to moneyed.
       Whose well-heeled,
       Snub monotonous mediocre.

Vanity.
A teapot's tempest.
Makes mountains by moles
       Ego-related.
Verily debated cliquish cliche.
Latent in its attraction to fault-finding
       By others, *Exclusive.*

Vanity.
Indistinguishable jibe.
Insults to injury, race-baits, contemporarily brocades
       With HATE speech, so many.
          Hideous in their derogatory wind
          From tundra's frozen, *Censorious.*

Vanity.
Necessary unnecessity.
Esteems esteem,
           Quality-Controlled.
Insinuates in affirmation, ill-conceived.
Deceives, by measure,
           To reassure the pleasure
                      Of *'Supreme!'*

Street

Comfort *wild.*
Taste the erstwhile dirt, destined ours.
    Growl, dogma! Howl!
Eat the meat
    Fresh from the edge of MENACING!
That, *humanity* become…tasty?
    Where there are children—playing?
    Grown-ups—praying?
Frantic about bloc-to-bloc [color] schemes
And legislations, should bullets rein back
    The truth about *belonging…*
Be it not, to concrete nor pavement,
Nor scarlet grass.

Color down! *Red.* Color down! *Blue.*
Color down, wheel of hue where *Black*
Does not *Yellow*, to *White.*
    Not in *this* alive!
Does not unfold a dollar's crease,
What value imbalances to custom-
    Ary care, for mixing
Social f[R]actions
    With money's decimal points.

Gangster down! *isms.*
At what cost should 'turf' be your 'hood'?
    Your not-so-misunderstood clamor
At intersections of corners named for people.
    Whiter. Blacker. *'Con'* Mexican descent.
Those Haves, Have-nots, Never-wills.
    Your not-so-simply, *numbers,*
Nomenclatured in [*barrios*] and [*projects*],
That *Crime*, by addition and subtraction,
Multiplies to percentages when watching Polls.

Relent! umbrellaed life's irony,
    That democracy burns generational,
The shackles from Mama's 'broke-ass' womb
    Up to her ineffectual tit,
Your comings and goings unsteady of age,
    And footing
The *bill* for being born
    To alms.

Go up, from bread and water,
Coffered per capita, the crumbs,
Portended by from what larder your family feeds.
    'Street,' plans the menu!
    Inherits the meek.

Whose [Housing Authority] brick tells the mortar,
        Keeps it, repeating:
            Without prejudice,

Shit of the equine!
[Because everybody loves a good animal story.]

Feral, is the polity, ill-suited for *good.*
Poses as chalk outlines,
    Whose brass, as old as Cain,
    Strews about asphalt, concrete as day!
And upon this malevolent frontier,
    Biased, in its shunting,
Suburb turns away,
Fealty's refugee,
    City.

Unflush, you turd!
That you continue your stink upon high hell, the demon, Privation!
    Poverty's bitch!
Whose 'bangers' ain't British, but monikered—tsotsis.
Barbaric in their approach to *pi*:
        Politically correct, in common uncommon dearth,
        The inhale of good air.

The Apology

Awash in guilt, four hundred years.
Up the river *James*—a ship.
Barnacled. Scraping bottom in its mangled 'body of Christ.'
Hungry, the victuals—in a cracker!—of Atlantic's trade.[25]
    Whose *Black-souls soup* crowned cotton 'King!'
    Tugged-o-unCivil War,
        Whose hooded legions, *caw! caw!*
      For crows name 'Jim.'
      Regulatin'.
      Segregatin'.
      Perpetuatin' myth
           That 'all' men, created equal,
           Ride astride broad shoulders common to *Masters*
             Long since dead.
             Rotted to compost's *Yesteryear,*
           Decayed in their culture-war jingo
             Erection to peat,
             Repeat.
           Repeat their slogans and praises,
           That 'Johnny' *will* 'come marching home again,'[26]
           With 'Jackson' yet unchained.
Because 'Rebecca' sure as hell, ain't leaving no farm,[27]
Running off with some city
    Slicker than molasses,
    And twice the dark!
       Sticky, when left uncovered
From oversight's *'ordinary'* care.

You are rebuked!
Rebuffed!
Box-stuffed and closeted with old shoes!

Let *Woke* be the Devil's bare feet!
    Propagandized political profit gone to blister.

---

[25] *History documents the first African slaves—initially sold as indentured servants, in return for food—were brought to Virginia on a European ship (Dutch) in late August 1619, one year before the Mayflower*

[26] *Reference to "When Johnny Comes Marching Home Again," written by Patrick Gilmore, 1863, upon the notion that soldiers returning from war will be met with great fanfare. Often mistaken as a song intended to solely soldiers of the Confederacy, it was equally embraced by soldiers of the Union Army.*

[27] *Reference to the Kat Douglas Wiggin's children's novel, Rebecca of Sunnybrook Farm, published 1903*

Eyes Only your 'inhospitable' Dixie,

> What disillusions you do
> These sixteen-more begats,
> Your first slaves' progeny.

"[N]animal Lovers!"

"Gets my goat!"[28]
    The flea catchers in this place.
Trampling all over my well-built, *'Eurocentric'* furniture!
Broken down, like my itemized tax deductions,
    Whose muster also must beg inquiry.

"Sticks in my craw!"
    The bologna given goose, by gander:
        The worm, 'for the birds!'
        Regurgitated.
Feeds on crow; calls it, 'chicken:'
    Free range in its rejection of disingenuous guilt
    For misdeeds of *race,*
    Reduced to *pulp fiction.*
        Book-banned and rewritten
        As *p[H]atriotism!*
And we are pithy in our sidewalk views,
Regarding dimestore chew,
    Spat about these aggregate hues.
Walking back, back, black
        To exclusion.
What poult be not *anothers* plate,
    'Wild-chased' nor 'loose.'
(Such bull's left-behinds,
    Battered and fried into greasy atmosphere,
Make flatulence upon good air, fascist!
    Subastral, in affairs of state
    And person.)

"Hold the reins!"
    The horse's ass.

Outrageous **Hate**! astride.

---

[28] *Expression of annoyance/anger, seeking redress. Said to have come from the idea that goats are typically brought into the stall of a temperamental thoroughbred to spend the night before the race, as a calming agent.*

Its bully pulpit:
    Anti-mixing, handicapped,
        By sermons, what
                Win
                Place
                Show
        Be *thoroughbred* afield *filly*.
    Judges <u>me</u>! Me! *Also-ran!*
            Pony!
Whose <u>one-trick</u>, is on me!
Whose comeuppance to *righteous* is 'in a pig's eye!'
    For lack of flying
    Straight and narrow.
            Perpendicular, on our horizontal plains.
"Weaseled out!"
    The elephant in this room.
    Given to rage about mice!
That overgrown rodent,
    Tiptoeing where 'marching' beck and calls.
Whose droppings,
    Sufficient to disturbance,
Traps and poisons our cheese-gullible
In pestilence borne thereof
    Where sleeping dogs lie.
    Where 'truth' wears canderous distortions,
            Toothy in its dripping rhetoric
What '*Best Regards!*' the pack of wolves
            Behind phobic's iniquitous door.

"And 'earnest' are we, to rule the roost
    — *"With welfare for all"* —
This chickenshit coop!"

Mixed Drinks

Sipping Sade[29] and <u>brown</u> whiskey
>In the <u>blackest</u> of countries,
Europe bellies up to the bar,
>Gets drunk on *white lightning*,[30]
Disparages the crudeness of oil,
>And razes Africa's roof to scorched earth,
>In perpetuity!

"To the ruins!" toasts Europe's leaded glass.
>Formal, in patent leather and bow,
>Tied to ballgown customs, and scents
>That smelled of Slavery,
>>Fast-forwarded to char's extant flame,
>Around what dances, *history*.
>>A mystery…exactly whose?

Given to cheer, dominion's guile.
Imbued in boast of bastions:
>*Truth*
>*Faith*
>*Freedom*.
Inebriated, cocksurely upon 'backward' hens,
>"Black-assed and begging for a rooster,"

That the *good egg*
>Be blessed the quickening sheen,
>Of *White light*.
>>Shown over this dark continent.
That biddies, and those who raise them,
>Stay cooped
>>In Geopolitic's chicken wire.
>Raped, pillaged, plundered.
>Unguarded by ivory's diamonds,
>>Centuries removed
>>By White men and their *burden*.[31]

---

[29] *Born Helen Folasade Adu in Ibadan, Nigeria, to a Nigerian father and English mother, Sade (pronounced shaw-dey)Adu has proved one of the most successful lead female singers in British music history.*
[30] *Illicit homemade whiskey (North America), typically colorless and distilled from corn. Romanticized as a much favored enterprise among those in rural or wooded locales in the America South.*
[31] *By definition, the responsibility European colonizers felt to impose their civilization over those of occupied countries in countries Brown and Black. Coined, "The White Man's Burden," 1899, Rudyard Kipling.*

Political, still, the flexible straw.
      Drink companion, preponderant.
Extravagant in its bold assertions
That linear is the world's round ways.
      Given over to 'discovered,' what has been stolen,
         Broken in its *Darkie* servitude
         To drunken governance
            And its unruly children.
[Their shackle and chain, yoked, generationally, neck-to-neck, from 'bad earth.']

Abundant in lore, this 'lie!'
      What—repeated—is the *Critical Race*.

      The loser in its lane
To affairs of *State* and franchise.
      Corrupt in its prejudiced republic(an) ash,
      With smoke of commerce
         That market the World.

The Avenue
(Or...What White Men are Really Afraid of)

She wore *spectator* pumps.
    Cherry-red and lilly-white.
Blush, begat forgotten times,
The roses her cheeks revealed.
    Anemic, in their subtlety
About the tinge, tint, tincture
Of *'outdoor'* life.

Into a yellow sun, her gait,
    Gliding agaze a slate-blue sky.
Men at Work (polychrome),
Framed squarely upon her to and fro,
Aside the green eyes,
    Of monsters.

Here and there—her mosey.
Along the variegated tans and olives,
    Browns and blacks,
Of *The Avenue*.
Where she adjoined herself
To more modest shoes, there mingling.
    Scuffed, in their daily heel-to-toe

    Of city's 'tribal'...
"Indivisible, with liberty and justice for all!"

Today, she is almond milk.
    Digestible to 'All'
    What color—*just enough*—be plenty white,
    To suckle the savage breast, 'Miscegeny!'
    Whose intolerant gut, labels her,
        "Wet...on dirt!"
    Refusing to call herself, *"mud."*
Centuries-thru, become the 'chocolate.'
    What color—*one* drop—be just enough
    To know that, then, she had
        ARRIVED!

Roombound, no more,
To ethnocentric pudding,
    What solitary 'vanilla' be bittersweet
    Unto us [unchefed] in *supremacy.*

And we are romantic,
In our notions of bigots and bastards
    Mothered to fatted calves
    Who refuse our *just desserts.*

Even with Wings...

Withdrawing from the ledge,
Where personal matters make ants
Of giants below,
Hope be of good sound,
To fear the heights.
Retreats into the security of *sameness*
That, suddenly, is no different
Than status quo of coaster rides
To Heaven.
Those ups and downs—sequentially.
Birthday-cake occasions counting years.
Months, days, and moments
NOT of cheer.

Of [what] feather,
This...*bird?*
'Pedestrian' asunder an urban sky.
Why, to *this* stage Auditions for crowds?
Becomes fodder, at dinner tables.
Suppositions unscripted:
Unrehearsed.
Unsolicited.
What plumage,
Ruffles to nauseous endurance,
The housekeeping of feeling '*Also-Ran*':
'Grounded.'
Peckish.
Constipated in thought
Of falling
To a chalk outline
On an unsuspecting ground.
Crowd-pleased!

None are the wiser, still.
Nor 'ample,' the explanations, thereof.
...But for the looky-loos,
Who, among them
Offer reasons,
Why *no one* knows my name,
But call me, *dodo!*

"Put a Cork in It!"

A cork cannot, a constant pour, abort
        What intoxication
        Fills politic's carafe.

   Could not,
        Should not
The *shite* of bulls, bottle.
        Name it, 'Fine Wine & Spirits,'
To quench the thirst,
        Argument.
Whereupon a box's slippery soap,
        His/Her sound-bite soliloquies.
Wrapt in what the mirror did not see,
        Or what, within a public's speaking,
        Makes mockery, his/her words
            'To live by,'
When furloughed from the sensitivities of the *ordinary*,
        To become *extraordinary*
        In his/her treasons.

To each, his/her platform!
And to each, a crafted *stump* of wood
        Veneer.
Some be, for truth-telling,
        What, into a megaphone, his/her timbre
        Proves, the *real*.

While others,
        Spring-mounted on *bendable* plane,
For from only jumping.

   To conclusions about *primacy*,
In a pool of unsortable citizenry.

'Elements' and their chemistries,
        That have nothing to do
With picks in toothless mouths
They serve!

Not So Subtle...

"The Great White Way!"
       These electric-light billboards
And playhouse marquee bricks and mortar.
Native to the 'District's' disregard
       For theater's less-of-wage,
       Advantage,
           And color.

Indeed!
Truth be, it 'was'
       That pre-LED *song and dance.*

And 'was' it, too?
That the only dark faces
       On review,
Unadorned in 'pancake' and costume,
       And epithets about *'Mammy,'*
Took the broom, that a family be fed.

Districted Broadway...
       Squarely confined
To Manhattan height, hype, and hubbub,
       Stays, in *Time*
       Illuminated by night,

       With what it wishes not seen,
           By day.

Culturally harlequin, this revelry.
Mesmerized in truth about color:
       What sneaked into the night—a thief!
       Relieved the amusement, cuckolded by the rich,
What cachet, found, was not lost, at all!
       Got lynched on the Mississippi River's edge.
       Got boobytrapped in an Asian jungle
           That had *nothing* to do with the ghetto.
       Got lost at the ballot box
           On occasions, 'equality' reached the 'floor.'

As EXIT is ENTRANCE to *offstaged* plays,
[Bad] acting, personifies
To negligent *Color*
   What has always been
   Translucent, at best.
Determined to stay…exclusive.

The *Way* be not [White] at all!
   But, be [gray], the people.
After curtains are drawn
   At home.

Yeast for the Foolhardy Baker

She prefaces her answers to my every question,
       "You remember I told you…?"
Which, if I do not, in my response,
       Her query's bus
Will, up my back,
       Make flatbread, my burnt buns!

She elaborates my persona,
       "The *milk* of toast," insists, she does.
That I am speechless about crumbs of 'better' men,
       Full, in her epicurean thrust into my heart,
That, *pro tem*, is her constancy
       Toward two, an oven, bake.

She spoons my victuals,
       Vaulted from Grandma's secret recipe.
Those, 'Rules and Regulations…'
Secreted by her spatulas and bowls,
       Which, employed, spreads manure,
       That [my] baking goes to shit!

She feeds me intrigues:
       Measured 'pinches' and 'dashes.' 'Cups.'
Her agency, in mixing and stir,
       Sends wood, among the mettle of metal,
Her whisk designed for fluffing egg.
       Beating to stiff, its peaks, its disapproving valleys.

She entreats me in Treaty.
       Treatise-licensed letters, amore.
That, *avant-garde* her prerogative of me, her garden,
       Plowed, tilled, harvested.
Treated the care of a 'muffin man.'
       Eaten daily.

Geography

Wonders one, about the 'movement' of hate…

North, South, East, West.

Coast to coast. Border to border.
Highway to byway. Setting to scene.
People of little, from people of means.

Corporate dogma, to *white elephant*; HOA to PTA.
"Good fences" for "good neighbors,"
To affability gone astray:
Race baiters!
Provincial commentators!

Truth & Justice unequally yoked,
That a hatred thrive.

Well…

↓

↓

↓

'Rest in Peace,'
America.

Wonders another, the reason why?…

"God Bless America," "America the Beautiful," "My Country 'Tis of Thee."

- Slept-in beds community, streetbound.
  Playground to playground, waft four hundred years strong
      The servile discontent
          What whip cracks *domain's eminence*.
              Imminent in backs bared impotent;
      What end smacks *urban renewed* from where 'white' has flown,
              Behind them, left a wretched place;
  What ploy its *gentrified bricks & mortar* reconstruct, Destructed in its own
                      rubble.
          Recycled, the dignity of City over Citizen.

- Border complexion 'Brown out':
      Corridors to northern lights,
      Upon whose army's frail shoulders fall,
  Belie the truth about bootprints,
      Marching on jingoist feet and custom.

- ♫ *" 'School to Jail '* [32]
      Raises bail
  Community has to pay!" ♫

- ***And why?...***   **'Supremacy Rule!'**

---

[32] *A criticism made toward the American education system, that reportedly implements policies and procedures that theoretically "funnel" targeted minority children out of public schools into the waiting arms of the ever-lucrative criminal justice industrial complex...JAIL!*

Not-So-Anonymous...

The slippery slope
Under a drinking man's walk,
Zigs and zags stone to stone,
The peopled corridor of forced sobriety,
Wet, in its conclusions
About his viability to rehabilitate
Self's conflicting deprecations.

Headlong, his improprieties
Swerve about the man of bygone ways,
Mounted [each], and walled
That *all* can see!

And witness, we,
The stench, the stain,
The sticky aftermath,
Intoxication's
Beer, Wine and Spirits.
And none is the wiser

That he has hoisted *many*
A precarious public life.
A beast of habit, must he,
Defined by a graph's lines,
Pulse an inebriated heart.
Flatlined by his future
Among tombstones, catacombs
And crypts.

No Walking Required!

Street Math for Tyrone

Summed up in algorithms,
The equations of myth…

Solved for x:
$$\underline{(+\text{'s and }-\text{'s}) \times 1^2 \div \text{by equity}}$$
$$= \text{Food Stamps,}$$
Public Housing,
The Achievement   Gap.

The calculus of *drive-by* policing—another thing.
          Everything to do with math.

●   *Impends upon the commonweal:*
Motley. Schismatic.
Ineffectually-*gifted* a nation
          Whose 'forward progress,' is stiffed to *stillness,*
Upon an ever-moving globe.

●   *Offends a Color's realm.*
          That, behind the wheel, are menacing [cars],
          Masquerading *community* 'partnership'
                    Behind what numbers call themselves, "data."
          'Protecting and Serving' streets-uncouth, as *policy.*
          Mixed variables—the *black and white* of things—revealed
                    To sobering conclusion:
                              $B = 5W\text{-}2.$
          Linear, in functionality for the few.
          Extrapolates to *decrease,* the many,

The angle of geometry,
          In billiards and in blight,
Calculates redemption in [Housing] of noble names:
Francis Cabrini, Robert Taylor.
          Pruitt and Igoe.
…Subsidizes the line-item purpose, what angles taken,
          To adjoin in nation, held captive
          On dilapidated grounds.

Linguistically formulaic, these charts and graphs,
These city's blueprints and backroom deals.
>> *Restored and balanced*
To the algebraic morass of capital venture.
>> Hemmed in so-public walls,
Our *dirty [big] secret,*
>> Unreliably kept.
Mathematically
>> Incorrect.

Money Matters!

His Common Cents...
>Did a *nickel*.
>Was 'rehabilitated.'
>Cleans at the local *Five & Dime*,
>Minimized in *manhood*
>And recidivism.

His Besiegement...
>Divested, the ladder, a wall to climb,
>Scuffed in parole, to *humble*.
>Exacted, from *upright* to flaccid,
>Limping about the ruins, *prosperity*.

His Bankruptcy...
>Hungry!
>In the high cotton of other's fields.
>Becomes the boll weevil's dinner.
>Flesh and blood FREE!
>A slave's wage that diminishes coin.

His Broke Ass...
>Camels have backs
>Susceptible to straw.
>A bushel makes it 'plenty!'
>Loads upon his truculent beast,
>A *burden's* contract to provide.

"All In"[33]1...
>Was accused of being *Black*.
>Fingered his chips, with the synchronicity of *whales*.
>Looked into "the whites of their eyes,"
>Drew to an inside straight,[34]
>
>And won!

---

[33] *When a poker player bets all of his/her remaining table stakes to secure his/her bet on a pot.*

[34] *In draw poker, an inside straight draw (also referred to as "gut shot draw" or "belly buster draw" because of its difficulty and low probability of success), is a hand with four of the five cards required for a straight, with the middle card in the sequence missing.*

Ain't Just Us!

Nappy boy!
  Who's your daddy?
     Negligent about
        Your *characteristic.*
        Your *linguistic.*
           Your sophistic retreats' retreat:
           Your Public School[-to-prison] pedigree.
           Your 'ghetto fabulous!' insecurity.
           Your liquor stores and *Corners.*
           Your Crips.
           Your Bloods.
                 Others, AK-like.
Barefooted in shoes,
Trained to perception's road unpaved.
        Along which hypocrisy injures to blisters,
        Riding shotgun to dearth, obesity's *desert food.*[35]
             Strategically placed.
             Surreptitiously cultivated in usury.
             Statistically perpetrated
        Upon the frozen tundra of *'dollar ascendancy.'*
Minimum-waged, sans a story's *rags to riches,*
        Charged the offense of being poor…
"Fits the profile." Takes the rap.
     "Onesie-to-Life!"
                 …For living!
Nary a damn day,
        For escalating up, downward mobility.
        Zigzagging the IN/OUT circular reasoning of difference.
             Why, persistent, the resistant CHANGE!
                 'Obama-esque.'

---

[35] *'Food Desert' is a socio-economic term that refers to an urban area, primarily inhabited by poor and/or underserved minority communities, where it is challenging, if not impossible, to find and afford any quality food—making available only cheap, unhealthy food fare for a targeted public's consumption.*

Straight away, this blue-eyed mane!
        Chantilly lace, and all…
Domiciled in *economy of scale*:
        [Fat] in fine dining—*Top Shelf!*
                "Makes a better *victim*."
                "Less likely, the thief upon a loaf,
                        That a slice or a crumb consoles"
                                        Your justice system at work!

The 'Other' Woman

I saw the lie
She beseeched her mirror to tell.
And I lied to her,
Too.

I sampled the fare served to her *truth*,
Spooned the broth, its complexity's simmering pot.
And fat I grew, socially malignant,
In her diffidence stew.

I fed her heartbreak, oats and grains,
When bread was my shoulder—upon which her hunger scolds.
And she horded me, my sensitivity
Toward her advice-free diet.

I drank her flimsy arrogance,
Sipped her serendipity in small quantity, as did she, mine.
And she responded with spew,
Into my drunken hands—cupped.

I painted her, *roses and chandeliers*,
Bathed her salts' sanguine aroma.
And she chafed,
At the notion that water bends face
At war with time…and with me.
I gave her, song, in trebles and clefs.
'Sing-a-long, sing alone togetherness.'
And she screeched
Show-tune fictions, upon my tone-deaf ears.

I accompanied her seductions—her reductions.
Her romance *flights of fancy*.
And she doubled over me, with dismissal,
My rocket's failed trajectory.
I marveled at her, as she dabbled in me.
And *we,* confined to ring fingers,
Schlepped through housekeeping—a broken vacuum,
Whose function, did not.

Quitclaimed By My Decades

Well, it's like, um,
>> Getting benched.
>>> A changing of the guard.
>>>> Being overlooked.
>>> Unsought-after.
>>>>> Replaced.
Obsolete.

It's like, uh,
>> Knowing bygone roads,
>> **Closed To Thru Traffic**
(And return visitors)
Sunrise to sunset.
>> 'All Traffic EXIT Right'
>>> To *after*.

Yeah, it's like, hmm,
>> The *new* tricks
>>> The old dog didn't learn.
>> Never will.
> While,
To *"That Whimsical Pup!"*
Goes the glory, *modernity*.
>> Eaten by the promise
>> Of my social [in]security.

It's like, well…
>> A curtain is drawn.
>>> Where voices from shadows and cats
>>> Are answered,
>>> To fortune tellers.
And other such salesmen
>> At my door.

The 'Rose' Misnomer

When pretext advantages her…

She, gardens blooms aplenty;
Grooms elegant men
    Among the noxious weed—*flirtation.*
Her spade, cultivates
    No finer amenities of tillage and seed,
        Designed for raising children in fertile soil,
    Produced.

She regards, highly,
The 'fertilizing' quality of horse and cow;
    Goat and sheep;
    Chicken—when the mood for eggs
        And uncandid acquaintances
Complement her habit
For meat and greens.

He is *dungarees and pretense*:
    Soils her mudroom and clothes receptacle.
    Scandalizes her perpetually soiled nails
        And propagates the smudged forehead & cheek,
        Her thorny roses reveal.
But, and when pretext advantages him…

She is malevolent in his misdemeanors and felonies.
    …The deeds and thoughts of madmen,
Broken to intransigence, her cost,
That *faithlessness* brings drought, her horticulture.

And she is, thenceforward, 'unflattering,'
    In her groundskeeping,
And unmovable in his guilt.

...Fell in Love with a Stripper

At the gate, the *frenemy!*
    She is accomplished
    In her nimbleness toward men.
(Grown hesitant in their wobbly *talents* upon women they indulge.)

Mildly, a man,
By conversant views,
                        He is
What some might say, milquetoast.
Illiterate to her moves.
        Her capture.
        Her supercilious penchant
            For *amateurs!*
(Those 'little britches' in *Men's Suits*, aimlessly about their window's shopping.)

And as such,
Dispatches he, the riches of reveal…
    That upon the urge he *make[s] it rain!*
    Rags are made, her reflected
        Self.
Attendant, her *woman,*
Magnificence on display.
    Her jewel.
    Her fabric.
    Her *je ne sais quoi,*
        Labeled, a profession-old,
    That makes camping soldiers
        Of gentlemen.
And gentlemen—the unkind.
When commences *she* what women do
    To egos dressed in rags,
Goes he
Into her 'mollycoddle.'
    Her *vector.*
His line of sight—her curves.
His fiber, straight and narrow,
        Descending,
Dripping from her tongue-
        And-groove construct.

In his *reveal*...
    The inequality of men.
        The size of *Men's Shoes*.
            Men's Gloves.
(Those exceedingly-tall, tall tales that men tell other men...about lying.)

She, by most account,
Is 'tender' flush.
    Spendable, only as coin,
    Baring all
        That men call *gold & silver*.

She is, therefore,
Well-accomplished in his sagging.
    Responds a siren's song,
    The premature reckoning
        Everyman sing.
And does, she,
    Brilliantly,
    Pretend what is, at most,
        His 'temporary' *fit*.
(Which, en[rich]ing, makes her indulgence, all things, 'pride.')

Ad Hoc Lives

The *'Flop*:
>Those,
>At leisure,
>In the daily *"grind,"*
>The nature of the incurious,
>Diligence-deferred,
>While standing
>Still.

The *'Runner-Up'*:
>Those,
>Extemporaneous.
>Driven to confessions
>About undependable attendance
>To *others* in constant pursuit
>The life, liberty, happiness,
>Negligently perused,
>In 'this' *American*
>History.

The *'Also-Ran'*:
>Those,
>Engineered,
>Puppeteered,
>Commandeered *Live!*
>In their living
>Colors.

The *'Ne'er-Do-Well'*:
>Those,
>Who hope
>Against hope,
>Get lost in the shuffle,
>A fair hand to bluff.
>Is called,
>A liar.

The *'Feckless'*:
>Those,
>Reckless of character,
>Whose labor's love went missing
>Among footprints of 'trifling,'
>Seen walking, on tiptoes,
>Among *losers*.

Mergers and Acquisitions

A *thing…*
    This wilderness of mergers and acquisitions.
Cultivates, in fields and streams,
    The unreciprocated love for fish, of fowl,
        Conglomerated,
    So that industrious men persevere,
'Planted' in indoctrination, as one thing,
    Bushwhacked,
Hijacked,
    By, yet another.

Pleasures the *haves,*
This 'hardwood love'…
    Deforests oak, ash, and beech,
    That cribs be 'tricked,' and rides, 'pimped'
At the patronage of *have-nots.*
    'BOGO' offers them softer wood,
What particle board pins up pictures
    Of low-born accommodation.

Big fish…small pond,
Into whose paths, swim minnows,
    Mom & Pop, in this 'American' dreaming,
Who become food for fodder
To arbitrage:
    Commoditized in timber and finny prey.
    Downsized to *Community Chest,*
        Constant in service
To the habitual avarice of amalgamation.

"Old money," *"new money,"*
    Whose blood be, now, *black,*
Unapologetically about Labor and Wages,
    At 'pecuniary advantage,'
    Wall Street's sword & shield.
        Worshipping the 'gap'
        Twixt a collar's colors.

(M&A), Last and least in,
First and most out.
This *Wilderness,* this *Wood,*
This *water's* determination
    For shares, *'preferred.'*
        'Voting' shares that make, so *'common'*
    The shares the unmonied.
Divested.

Suburban Respite

Fatigues to poverty,
 Does urban life.
Tires to proximate despair engulfing me
 In constant blemish,
A soiled landscape permits.
 …The 'housed,'
 Under authority of City.
Causes *White* to flight.
 Circling high, the promise of 'One Nation…'
Only to look down its flared nostrils,
At stinking municipalities of the lessened.
 "Renewed,"
 "Rejuvenated,"
 "Refurbished."
Revitalized to irrelevance
 In election polls and TV sweeps.
Dyslexic *likes* of media's social nature,
 And other disreputable data
That stays well, in print.
 Out of the mouths,
 Of robots
Standing guard, my planned community's gate.
Against the mother city's propensity
 For unplanned pregnancies.
  (Those baby mamas,
Daddy dramas.)
 And other failure to thrive
 American dreams.

The Bitch That is Denial

Ash-in-mouth[36] as she is,
Her conceits in 'self'
Remind the cloud,
How prominent is the rain
That a parade cancels.
Drenching platitudes
With *buckets* of 'cats and dogs,'
Upon my parched earth—cracked to curls.
Resistant to propagation.

Exposes skeletal remains,
Her horn's toot.
Self-inflicted
By her mirror,
Too blind to see
Her smudges, cracks, and chips.

She is self-congratulatory,
Nonetheless.
Condescending in her ascending nose,
Sitting atop turned-down lips
That make gargoyles of cherubs
In love.
But, bridesmaids
Of sycophants,
Social monogamists,
And others 'divorced' from her relevance.

---

[36] *As defined by idioms.thefreedictionary.com, "To become sickeningly disappointing;*
to go from being a source of joy or hope to one of despair or anger."

The Less Said...

Her disappointment, she does not share.

     Except in love letters, she does not write,
     Texts, she does not answer,
     Wishes upon starry skies, she does not make.

    Becomes disapproval.
    Dismissal.
       Dismal (he) in her shunting.
       Her struggle
            With deed,
            Over the idle word of water.
Although, fortified, is he, in his *barking* wood,
       Petrified at the thought,
       Her river ebbs and flows.
Until, on the rocks,
Fells *insecurity's* most stubborn of trees!

And he,
       The perennial *hugger*,
          Reclused from her approval,

For apoplectic forestry,
Is felled.

A Primer

Settled, in this amniotic sac,
Female bantam[37] waits, shoved about,
Larger male—her twin.

Gestation[38] actual…
       Pushed out, taken-in, is she,
              The moment's 'quintessential' *hustle:*[39]
That she is [gone] into the confidence of pigeons,
       Who, like [she], have flown a coop,
              Into the footprints of other 'birds,'
              With feather and down
       Whose 'petite' becomes 'minuscule,' 'nanoscale,'
              'Naught.'
       Whose glass ceilings[40], misogynist[41] minions
              And biased genderisms, other,
       Cause her perpetual position
              "Behind the eight ball,"[42]
A game that she has never played,
       But is always subject the loss.

---

[37] *'Bantam' refers to a person quite small, as compared to others, and prone to fight, if necessary.*

[38] *'Gestation' is defined as the period in the womb, from conception to birth.*

[39] *'Hustle' is a slang term, in this case, for a person doing what he or she does to survive.*

[40] *'Glass Ceiling' is a term used to indicate that women and girls are challenged advancement, due to attitudinal or organizational biases and constraints.*

[41] *'Misogynist' refers to a person who dislikes, despises, or is strongly prejudiced against women.*

[42] *'Behind the eight ball' is a phrase that applies to a person who finds themself at a distinct disadvantage for success at something.*

Forty-Five

Man alive!
Who'd uh thunk, from a rat's ass,
Could foulness, so toxic a wind,
Grift infamy into dollars, in a bank's accounting [of] fraud;
And bilk reputation of Party (once, of *milk n honey*),
Now, clabbered, and lactose-overdosed
To outcomes
Most shitty!

Holy cow!
And the creek *did* rise!
When came to past,
That '16 offense,
Furthered down his primrose path.
Until *contemporariness*
Has its way in opinion's court.
Liar-courted, that hoards be pugnacious
About *primacy*,
Supreme in its unraveling.
Going backroads,
Where Jim Crow become John Birch.
Become…

OMG!
Beats everything…
The 'Oval' antics in this place.
Corrupt, in their bargains with the devil,
In whose details is a desert,
Open to corporate pleasure, those rich, and richer still.
Obsessing, in social media's crotch,
The urge to become *bigger* than the less 'eclectic.'
Those serfs,
Acquiescent to his presence.

I'll just be damned!
Bedlam!
What mountains of dirt slung,
Have become mud,
A *Hill*
Eroding.

Horse Shit!

My earlier oats,
Unsettles to gaseous complaint.
    When, up next to me, sidles a goat!
        Elucidating the 'stench' of *my* manure
        Side by side *his* virtually orderless,
    And beneficial…poop!
Très élégante!

"Horseshit!"
        Neighs my knockback to his own regard.
"Would it be that your meat,
        Your milk,
            Your *more,*
Betters my galloping?
My sport of kings,
    Domiciled in majesty,
        That leisure and company
        Value (your) association
In a finer way?"

To which is the billy's
    "Nay, must you neigh?
    When amour propre be my way,
    And 'old goat' becomes me."

Consequently…
    And certainly not inconsequentially,
Is my hindquarter hoof,
    In shoes,
To his horned butting-in.

Capitol Ideas

Lately,
Lotta 'testifying' going on!
      Not about Jesus or Muhammed;
      Not about Abraham, about Buddha,
      Nor about whomever
         Claims the deity *du jour*—this secular place.
      Not about Mormons, or Catholics,
         Protestants or Jews,
      But the *chargé d'affaires*
         Whose state ambassadorships counsel
            These Disunited States,
        America.

But, aplenty about that, secular.
      Rumored in mills as *Pro* this
Or that, with 'much ado about nothing' to do,
      With <u>diversity</u> itself,
But run, adversely amok
The White [marble], a bicameral House—divided.
Going backward, the escalator 'UP.'

On the Matter of 'Size'...

The size of a person changes the landscape about him
What bends to the incautious winds and waters heavens-sent.

    He is wiry.

Muscular in his approach toward men,
Sinewy in his sensitivity, with women
Who have little sense, his unsuitability.

    She is **woebegon** in disapproval.
Fatigued, his 'swashbuckling' ways,
    Impetuously about her [yellow] rose.

But, steadfastly, *they* persist:
Harum-scarum—his ways.
Transcendent—hers.

Even so, *theirs* is the way of gorges and canyons:
    Craggy, deep,

        And bound to get each other
        ...Hurt.

Man's Best...

By necessity, his job;
When it suits him, his wife;
As required, his children
     (Their Christmases, birthdays, and Little League);
But never, the time given leave to,
That God might comfort, give.

At all times, his dog!

Far too frequently, his bartender;
Many mornings in transit, his donut shop;
Every now and then, himself
     (His blackjack dealer, cocktail waitress, and cashier);
But rarely, his pastor.

At all times, his dog!

Most times, his morning paper;
Here and there, his late-night TV;
More often than not, his social media
     (The chatrooms, platforms, and apps);
But "when pigs fly!" his family.
At all times, his dog!

"By Appointment Only," his primary care provider;
Annually, his weight;
In between the laughter, his grimacing
     (Those breakdowns, unreported);
But never—though decades, shed—his tears.

At *all* times, his dog!

Man, On Nature...

'Hook, line, and sinker'
The speckled trout swims away
A skillet laments

Gardeners adore
The *fly-away* ladybug
Aphids run amok

The brawling couple
Made a mole build a mountain
Where once there were plains

Searching for answers
The curious cat was killed
When drowned in the truth

Impulsive poultry
Regularly lay their eggs
On somebody's face

So 'dirty' the rat
Whose behind could not care less
How dank, is his hole

A pigeon comes home
Tired of scavenging parks
A stool awaits

Flutter you monarch
By human 'flights of fancy'
Scribbled in the sky

Crow walks on the face
Scarecrow stands in farmer's field
Straight does the crow fly

Frogs take 'leaps of faith'
Dogs fight in the deadly skies
When Man is about

Roosters rule the roost
Until dinner rings a bell
The hens cannot hear

In search of a life
To the Circus went a flea
Who found a sideshow

Seeing he was not
"Snug as a bug in a rug"
He vacuumed his house

Deep is the *Ant Farm*
Where human labor requires
Neither horse nor plow

The Heart Wants What
the Heart...

Whimsical!
    Failure's letters of love to its own success.
Stamped, *Romance...*
    'Lost in the mail' to middlemen with PhDs
And cures,
    "Handle[d] With Care," in her mirror's distress.
Written with avolition in his prose.
    Gathering regrets
Toward consequences unintended, about her fading
    Tattoos.
Discolored to envy's green,
    Designed for coveting
What becomes the *bile* of yearning.

Through her veins, his indifference.
    Coursing in pen and ink's indefensible tome:
The abuses of words,
    Scribbled in nouns, adjectives, and verbs
Posing as gerunds and participles,
    Past, present, and *future,*
Among browbeaten delusions of fools' wives
    And widows.

Impotent of good word, and of paltry romance,
    Dances, he, around who cavorts
With fidelity's bumptious claims
    That, *"Once upon a time"* was her heartbeat
    For men, gentle, *less* peckish than he.
    He, of late—the murmur.
Of arrhythmic guarantees fallen to science,
    In stents and in pills.

To overcoat and boots—retreat!
    That, against his torrential [reign],
Her temperate flame, vanquished to cinder,
    Remembers but, the singed white remnants of fire,
Extinguished to the ash of cruel neglect,
    Those things familiar
To loss. To losing. To love.

Proof-positive, the idle hands.
     Strangled of aptness, for having fingers.
Climbing fingers…
     Up-rope to Earth.
Whose grave is matrimony.
     Dirty, in phalangeal resolutions
Drunkenly, at midnights' annual flings
     Onto the scrapheap of disingenuous flirtation.

The Melted Pot

Let us now
Call our attention
    To the *"Cheesemonger,"*
Whose lactating herd
Milks *cow-sheep-goat* constituency,
Constipates to disagreements
    About texture, taste, recipe
What doctrine delivers class struggle.
Wayward Greece and Rome,
Into our contemporary
Kettle.

    Tricked into idiom,
    And "on its belly,"
Marches boot and bayonet.
    Uniformed Party.
Uninformed about lactose's intolerant disposition,
    The explosive 'diarrheal dairy' of *Rule.*
Maneuvers constant,
Through *Army's* ruminant bladder.
    Coagulate casein intrusion,
    Upon the gut,
Community less-fed.
    That, bitter fruit are born unguarded trees.
Rooted in hardscrabble,
'Republican'
Dirt.

'Gut-busted!'
    We vintner class *accomplices:*
    Cosmopolitan palates at worship, the altar—*cuisine.*
Of gastronomical similitude,
To foot and hoof of 'bitchy' types…
    Hauteur, atop the peckish,
At cantonment soirees and *feed.*
    Observing (in medals) campaigns pretended.
Horizontal, in belly.
    Upright-ish, head to toe.

Mice to traps, the *Charge!*…
    To cracker-thin baguettes
Garrisoned in grape, apple, and pear *Commons.*
    Where, about the melon and skin-encased charcuterie,
    Disperses the wooded swords' delight:

All cheer the 'melted' pot,
What fondues galvanize, cut-of-meat, fringe elements,
Whose tendencies of cheeseboard 'miscellany'
Becomes *inclusion's* 'foreign' amalgamation:
    That of butterfat, bacteria, and mold.
Pasteurized, naturalized,
    Neutralized to high-fat—under the gown of *Lady Liberty*,
In her [uncommon] forbearance
Of our 'ingredients,'
"Homogenized!"

Ain't melodramatic,
(What aristocrats do).
    Those Brie, Camembert, Gruyère.
Their cheesepared dominion, over knock-off spreads
    (And processed *foodstuffs*)
Domiciled in pressurized cans, and plastic tubs.
"Unsuitable," to cheesecloth-and-rind types.
    More discriminating, still, the grotto, 'grated' community.

So, cheese be *cheese;*
    And stuff be *stuff.*
Though the twain shall seldom meet,[43]
'Tis certain not in comity each other!

---

[43] Adaptation of Rudyard Kipling's *"Barrack Room Ballads" 1892*

Dodgeball for Beauty

Photographs are *made* to live
    As strangers, we had never met.
Except for on landscapes, prearranged.
    And in unfrequented amusement
At arcades and front-room mantels.

They come as thieves, absconding years
    Attributions provisioned the young.
What time has lapsed, to of 'little use.'
    Kept for itself, in diminishing
Celluloid *bits & pieces*—framed.

Forgotten faces, ear-to-ear
    With 'cheeses' tolerant lactose.
Worry-free about *wrinkle-free.*
    And other notions ill-conceived
By beauty's discreet *mascara.*

"See here, a midriff," proportionately
    'Skinny' in slender sustenance.
Prominent, the tribal *coif*
    Tags along years, to baldy distress
Combed over discarded time.

'Caught on film,' a *camera obscur[ed]*
    Flips the script, the histrionics.
Salvageable, only in pictures
…Common to change, what the pinhole sees
When searching for something, lost.

"Yes, Hipster, There Is Life After 30!"

Grieved '65.'
Until '70,' did agonize the news:
  "Time, is Winged!"
The years I'd shed. And feathers, too!

'Nifty' [*was*] '50.'
Though '60,' stalked, so near ahead.
    Constant, in acquaintance
With prescriptive refills
    Of pills,
And proof against solitary confinement.
Cadence to seven,
    Pill against the plastic—my daily
Times ten.
        Tick, tick.
        Tick, tick.
        Tick, tick, tick.
Day to day.
    Month to month.
    Year to year.

"Lordy,
[Came to grips with] Forty!"
Set '20' and '30' side by side.
    Interred with mementos of less regrettable times,
The decades hence.

It's Naval!

Family Dining the Dessert
That Spoiled Supper

Behind the civility of embrace,
      Crouching,
Resurrecting thoughts inharmoniousness in wait,
      The sneaking thief
Disguises kinship, with songs upon acrimony.
      Clan-extended—at *gatherings*
Of meat-n-potatoes, clawed from their throats,
      Startled to truth about blood, "thicker than water,"
      Pawned for pennies, the dollar begrudged,
To please discordant tastebuds
Of prodigal dysfunctionality, naked!

Reciprocal lunging forward, convivially,
      Forages, the *lambs to slaughter*.
Partakes of them, after dinner,
      To sweets' tooth.
Forked over consideration
"Left for dead."

Cheer and goodwill, becomes *kibble*,
      Disenchanted of spirit.
Gone hither and yon to neighboring suppers,
Clangorous, in their naked babel,
Bruising, in raw regard,
      Predicaments and quandaries,
Of relatives near
      And (kept) far.
Gorged, in belly,
      And liquor-loosed,
Prodigal sons & daughters, in-lawed & out.
Familiar strays—barking.
      At passing platters and gravy
      Boats.
…Shitting, where they eat.

      Be damned, what others eat!
Lays to waste, a *family* feed,
      The revelry,
Kinship's charred,
And 'broken' bread.

So periodic, the victualling,
	Of these *wolves*.
Vicious, in rumor and innuendo,
	Unscathed by whispers
Returning home.

The USS Salvation:

"All aboard!"
To the best part of me, became 'all' of me
Who swabbed the deck, my captainship's neglect.

"Ship ahoy!"
Tears on my table, because I could not deny
Every sad song my record player.

"Anchors away!"
T'ward distant ports-o-call, I christened you,
That of sailors—drunken or otherwise—you let sail.

"Shiver me timbers!"
The tree stump village I shelved you,
That no piracy prevail upon our turbulent sea.

"Into the deep!"
*   Me hearty, of 'bristol fashion,'*
Who, until my watery end, uprights me with caring.

'Casual Men with Children'

"Deadbeat!"

"Sperm Donor!"

"Baby Daddy!"

Wastrels all!
From my provisioning
    This cast-off army.

Carnalized,
From *casual* to *illegitimate,*
    In their baby mamas' single-parenting.

Relegated to 'second-handedness,'
    That I am the harm done by rats
    Unto their pantry.
(Customarily graced, the meager grains of salt,
    Onto their hunger's belly
        Wounds.)

I am, too, the *itch.*
    Flea-burdening the hopes
Of Infants & Children.
    Women.

And doggish, we men,
    'Lost' to them.
Gone *bush* to *bush,*
    Pissing!

Impregnating *good earth*
With the stink of strays
    On the soles of decent shoes.
(Black shoes, Brown shoes.
    The occasional White),
Esoterically among footwear's scuffed nature,
    A messy closet reveals.

The 'Attachment-Theoretical' Conundrum

Open—bares one's soul,
To the proximity of infatuation.
      Compromisable *sucker!*
   Is said, most likely
To welcome attachment's
      Shiny objects,
Penciled-in, to media's social
      Likes/dislikes,
People, Places, and Things
      [Algorithmic].

'Met,' 'Frequented,' 'Drawn to'
…The delicate art, of drawing lines,
      Of, sometimes-*friendly,* circles.
And *lovers.*
      And *others,* geometrically complex.
"Complicated," in *generosity*
      T'wards heart's ache.

Begs relief, this solitaire's redress.
That freehand adjuster to *Self,*
      Who makes mirrors distort
      Why *God* made reflection.
Opportunity goes to 'New!'
'Fresh!' ill-fitting *conformity.*
      'Convenient,' to triangles,
      Rectangles and squares,

Who know no better, than to conjoin
With disfigured support,
      Emotive to flight.[*]

---

[*] *Author's personal spin on the 1980s psychological Attachment Theory, found in adult relationships—whether acquaintances, close friendships, work relations, situational codependencies, or matters of romance—as inherently transitory in love and abandonment.*